The

Heav

Be Happy

Syd Little has been in the entertainment business for some forty years. Best known as one half of the comic duo Little & Large, his story is told in *Little Goes A Long Way*, published by HarperCollins.

Chris Gidney is an entertainer and writer. He is founder of Christians in Entertainment and is the author of a number of biographies of show business stars, including Harry Secombe and Frank Williams, immortalized as the Vicar in *Dad's Army*.

Michael Counsell, recently retired from parish ministry, is a veteran collector of church jokes. He is also the author of books of prayers and travel guides, including 2000 *Years of Prayer*, *All Through the Night*, *Every Pilgrim's Guide to the Journeys of the Apostles* and *Every Pilgrim's Guide to Oberammergau*, all of which are published by the Canterbury Press.

The Little Book
of
Heavenly Humour

Syd Little

with Chris Gidney
and
Michael Counsell

CANTERBURY
PRESS
Norwich

Text © in this compilation Syd Little, Chris Gidney and
Michael Counsell 2002
Illustrations © Rob Portlock, Mary Chambers,
Rob Suggs and Ron Wood 2002

First published in 2002 by the Canterbury Press Norwich
(a publishing imprint of Hymns Ancient & Modern Limited,
a registered charity)
St Mary's Works, St Mary's Plain
Norwich, Norfolk NR3 3BH
Second impression

British Library Cataloguing in Publication data

A catalogue record for this book is available
from the British Library

ISBN 1-85311-483-9

Typeset by Rowland Phototypesetting Ltd,
Bury St Edmunds, Suffolk
Printed in Denmark by Nørhaven Paperback A/S, Viborg

Contents

Introduction

A serious look at laughter

Did you know that having a good laugh today could actually increase your life expectancy? Music can sweep through the spirit and bring tranquillity to the soul, whilst drama sharpens the emotions and challenges the brain. Laughter, on the other hand, is God's perfect medicine. It's his provision for stress relief.

Laughter can turn tears of sadness into cries of joy, heaviness of heart into happiness of spirit, and in the middle of our difficulties remind us that life really does go on. Even the top medical scientists now claim that a good chortle has an enormous effect on the way we live our lives.

Fiona Castle said, 'The funniest times were when Roy was ill and was able to laugh at his illness rather than let it overcome him. So it is in life, it's often the difficult things that we laugh at later. If life really goes smoothly, you've actually got nothing to look back on and laugh at. If, for example, a wedding party goes smoothly it's often forgotten quickly, but if the wedding cake falls over you remember it and talk about it forever. It's the things that go wrong that are the funniest.'

I agree with Fiona and remember that when we were filming some sketches for our *Little & Large* television series for the BBC, it was always the unintentional events that caused the film crew to holler the most. On one occasion the script called for me to be lying on a beach when Eddie was to pretend that he was bored and request that he bury me in the sand. I was supposed to agree reluctantly, and the next thing the viewer was supposed to see would be Eddie driving a huge tractor with the hopper full of sand ready to dump on me. That was the essence of the gag, and visually it promised to be very amusing.

Looking back, I'm sure the good Lord was looking after me, as I had a strange foreboding feeling about it. I refused to do the sketch without the use of a dummy in my place. The Director was naturally disappointed, but I'm glad I insisted.

When the ton or so of sand was dropped on to the dummy, lying there happily in my place, it knocked all the stuffing out of it in an instant. All you could see was a huge cloud of dust, where I would have been lying. What was worse, the tractor driver had not fastened the front stabilisers properly, with the result that when Eddie pulled the lever, they came crashing down on the poor dummy's legs, and cut them clean off!

We all had a great laugh, and it made a very funny sketch, but my own amusement was tempered by the realisation of the close shave I had experienced!

In this book, I have tried to include as many true stories as possible, proving that truth is indeed stranger and funnier than fiction.

In a world of stress, pressure and uncertainty, laughter provides a unique way to switch off from life's everyday burdens. It's not a running away from problems however, as most jokes are focused around humanity itself. The slip on the banana skin, the mistake that someone made and the silly situations we find ourselves in become the focus of our amusement. Humour can help us face our fears, and see things as they really are with an uncharacteristic armour of confidence.

When I am invited to talk about my own personal struggles and how my faith helped me through, I ensure that laughter always has a central role to the evening. Those mirth makers whose job it is to create amusement have been entrusted with a seriously important gift. My good friends Cannon & Ball, Jimmy Cricket and Don Maclean recently joined me in making a video called *The Laughter Makers* in which they talked about how seriously they take the job and privilege of making people laugh. As Thomas Merton put it: 'Clowns and Comedians are likely to have a high place in heaven as they must be near the heart of God.'

So, does God laugh? The Bible says he laughs at the wicked and their feeble plans. Ecclesiastes says there is a time to weep and a time to laugh. Even dear, suffering Job longs for the day when God will fill his mouth with laughter once more. I'm sure that for Jesus to hold an audience of over five thousand men, as well as their women and children, all day, he must have used humour as a vehicle to get his point across. We remember what we laugh at because a joke demands a response. Jesus was an expert at driving home his points with terrifically funny gags of the day. I wonder if the disciples were the original 'Crazy Gang' or 'Riding Lights Theatre Company'? Did they engender hoots of mirth as they enacted the man trying to get a speck of dust out of his brother's eye whilst unable to see the log sticking out of his own?

The Bible says that we should have the attitude of little children in order to enter Heaven. Whenever I am with children they seem to spend most of their time laughing. So perhaps we should take a leaf out of their book too?

We're pretty adept at judging each other in church so maybe we could practise changing our piety for humour. I heard a story about a couple who were on the way home from church, standing at the bus stop waiting in the torrential rain for over half an hour. Finally they decided to pray for help. It was good to put into practice what the sermon had been about that morning, they decided. Bowing heads and closing eyes they began to focus their thoughts directly heavenward. As they prayed with outright fervour and confidence they didn't hear or see the bus arrive, stop and then promptly leave without them. Opening their eyes just in time to see it pull away round a corner they elbowed each other back into consciousness as they suddenly remembered the dual command from the preacher's revelation of Jesus in Mark 13 when he said '*Watch* and pray'!

Of course there are different kinds of laughter. The laugh bellowed in scorn does not have the same birthplace as a laugh of fun and jollity. Like everything in God's perfect creation, laughter can be twisted and used to bring harm rather than healing. God used his words to create the world in Genesis, so let's use our words to build up rather than tear down. Perhaps the main issue

Introduction

is to laugh *with* someone rather than *at* them. Laughter has been given to us as a tool of communication, not as a way of hurting someone.

Similarly, we should not find ourselves laughing at God, but recognise that he laughs at our crazy attempts to subdue life, whilst still loving us deeply. Ultimately God's desire is for our laughter to be the outward expression of the deep love and security we can experience from him. Whilst we should not expect to be bubbling with superficial laughter all the time, every true Christian can be full of deep joy.

There are three aims for this book. One is a reminder to take our faith seriously, but not ourselves. Being a serious bunch of humanity we could remind ourselves that it's important to see the funny side of our faith and our problems from time to time, but remember the fine line between laughing *at* someone and laughing *with* them. Let's not make fun of each other, but encourage one another to giggle, and see God chuckle with us.

The second is to provide illustrations for speakers, and to be a resource in getting the message across. Every gag has a moral attached.

The third is to encourage us all to take a dose of medicine for our own well-being. I've asked some of my show business mates to help. I'm thrilled that Bobby Davro, Billy Pearce, Rick Wakeman, Ted Rogers, Paul Daniels, Jim Davidson, Cannon & Ball, Don Maclean, Frank Carson, Jimmy Cricket, Wyn Calvin and a host of others have all given me their contributions. The result is a heavenly blend of my favourite jokes and true stories, guaranteed to make you chuckle. Michael Counsell, a Church of England priest and a veteran collector of church jokes has also contributed to this collection.

So, open these pages, open your mind, and prepare yourself for the best medicine on earth ... a hearty laugh.

Syd Little
May 2002

Holy Halos

Vicars and ministers create the fun

Laughing helps. It's like jogging on the inside.
Ken Dodd

Vicars are often at the centre of much hilarity, and sometimes they get their own back.

A vicar bought a horse from a local farmer, who gave him instruction in how to get the best out of his animal.

'If you shout "Praise God,"' the farmer explained, 'the horse will move off at great speed. To get it to stop you just have to shout "Amen!".'

The vicar thought this was great and paid for the horse before climbing aboard and shouting the command to get the horse to move off. No sooner had he echoed the words 'Praise God' than the horse set off at breakneck speed. They climbed hills; they sped along valleys and jumped fences.

Very soon they drew close to the village where the vicar lived. 'Slow down boy,' commanded the vicar. Nothing happened. 'Whoa there!' he ordered. Nothing. With a panic, the vicar suddenly realised he had forgotten the word needed to bring the animal to a halt. Faster and faster they went, the new owner hanging on for dear life.

Suddenly the vicar realised that they were way past his village and heading for the coast. Not only that, but they were heading for the coastal pathway and the cliffs beyond. Panicking he started to shout all manner of words in an attempt to find the missing word. 'Close Sesame! Open Sesame! Thanks be to God!' he screamed in desperation as the cliffs came in sight.

Suddenly he remembered it. 'Amen!!' he shrieked, and the horse stopped two inches from the edge of the cliff. He had been saved, but only in the nick of time. Gratefully, the vicar took a handkerchief from his pocket, mopped his sweat laden brow and exclaimed 'Praise God . . .'

Vicar: Can you all hear me at the back?
Voice: Yes, but I don't mind changing places with someone who can't!

After a short while, they simply accepted Hugh as one of them.

Holy Halos

The vicar came into church to begin his formal liturgy, but had a habit of tapping his microphone to make sure it was on. This week there was no sound coming back through the speakers, so he said, 'There is something wrong with this microphone!' Thinking the vicar had started his liturgy, the congregation obediently replied, 'And also with you.'

Our preacher's sermons always have a happy ending. The minute he ends, everyone's happy.

A minister was very proud of his idea for a new glass-fronted baptistery.

The money was raised, and the new pool built to the vicar's own specifications. Sadly, the glass cost so much that there was no money left for any changing rooms. The vicar didn't mind. They could complete the job later, and surely it was better that the glass gave his congregation a clearer view, he reasoned. A small wooden screen was hurriedly erected to protect the modesty of those being baptized.

The day to try out the new pool soon arrived. One after another the eager respondents took turns to get 'dipped', quickly moving behind the screen to change out of their wet clothes.

As the last of the men emerged from the glass tank, one lady started to panic. She had been worried from the start but now she was terrified.

3

Although starting to shake uncontrollably, she obeyed the order to begin her descent into the water. Suddenly her foot slipped on the marble steps, and as she began to tumble into the water, she seized hold of the only thing she could to try and break her fall. Unfortunately the screen she grabbed had not been properly secured, and as it fell into the baptistery it revealed three nude men drying themselves off.

The extremely red-faced men reacted fast in the best way they could think of, and jumped into the water to hide their nudity. They had forgotten that the baptistery was made of glass.

As the congregation doggedly continued to sing 'Just As I Am, I Come To Thee', they were treated to the sight of three nude men and one very confused lady, swimming around in the transparent pool, believing they couldn't be seen.

★　　★　　★

You can quit smiling now, dear – we're home.

An armless man applied for the job of bell-ringer at the church. Showing the man round the bell tower, the vicar carefully questioned him. 'Excuse me asking, but how do you intend to ring the bells without any arms?' he enquired.

At this the man stood bolt upright and banged his head in turn against each one of the bells in exactly the right order.

'Wow! That's simply amazing,' said the astonished vicar.

'Thank you,' replied the armless man, who took one step backwards and fell straight out of the tower window.

Running down the stairs to the ground floor the vicar found the man dead on the pavement. Just then a passer-by asked, 'Who's that man, vicar?'

At which point the vicar looked up and said, 'I don't know, but his face rings a bell!'

A minister was in a church where there was a strong policy on not drinking alcohol. One day he was visiting a lady who was bottling cherries from her garden in very strong brandy. She said that she would like to give the minister a jar, but because of the church's policy, that was difficult. She didn't want to do anything underhand. But then she thought and suggested that she could give him a jar if he promised to acknowledge it publicly. The minister accepted with grateful thanks. The next week's notice sheet contained this notice. 'The minister would like to thank a member of the congregation for a very kind gift of fruit, and the spirit in which it was given'.

The hospital chaplain visited every patient in the ward until he arrived at the last bed, where an oriental person was looking very poorly. As the chaplain watched he noticed that the poor man seemed to be getting paler and worse. He then stammered out a sentence before lapsing into unconsciousness. The patient's dying words were 'Ye yong wing ho marney di-en-poo'. The chaplain kept on repeating this to himself, thinking it might be very significant. He might have been entrusted with the last wishes of a dying man. But what did it mean?

Walking along the street, he pondered as he passed a Chinese take-away and decided to pop in and ask the man behind the counter if he knew what 'Ye yong wing ho marney di-en-poo' meant. The man laughed aloud and translated the words: saying, 'You silly old fool, you're standing on my oxygen tube!'

'Our jobs are quite similar,' said the bus conductor to the vicar. 'We ring bells, take money, and tell people where to get off.'

As part of a new drive to encourage more social activities, the vicar decided to hold a fancy dress party.

On the day of the party, there were all sorts of church

members in different costumes. Batman stood in one corner and Spiderman in another. Whilst the party was in full swing there was a knock at the door and in walked a man with a woman hanging down his back.

'Excuse me, but do you realise you have a woman hanging round your neck?' enquired one of the guests.

'Oh yes,' replied the man, 'she's my girlfriend.'

'But this is supposed to be a fancy dress party,' explained one of the other guests.

'Yes, I've come as a snail,' came the reply.

'What do you mean?' the guests asked.

The man pointed behind at the woman hanging down and said, 'That's Michelle!'

★ ★ ★

I think the deaf interpreter is ad-libbing again.

★ ★ ★

A church that occasionally invited guest preachers knew there was a man in the area who had a great reputation

7

as a brilliant speaker, so they decided to invite him for their Church Anniversary. However, when the man came he was terrible! He spoke for barely five minutes. He stuttered. There were long pauses and silences, and the enunciation of his words was appalling.

The deacons discussed this long and hard. They were shocked – especially as people spoke so highly of him. But, very graciously, they decided that he had had a bad day, and they would give him another opportunity to redeem himself. So he was invited to speak at the next year's Church Anniversary.

This time he was not brief as requested, in fact he went on and on. He spoke for over an hour without a pause for breath. It was long and rambling and full of red herrings. The Church Secretary could contain himself no more, so he approached the preacher afterwards and asked for an explanation. 'The first time you come to us you are brief and stumbling, the second time you seem as if you don't know when to stop.' The preacher was very embarrassed, but said there was a reason for his behaviour. He explained, 'The first time I came to you, I forgot to put my false teeth in. The second time, I accidentally wore my wife's set'!!

The family invited Granny to stay for a bit as she had not been very well and was not expected to live for long. The family were not in the habit of going to church, but Granny was a very devout Christian. The oldest child was home from university getting ready for exams, when she noticed Granny was sitting downstairs reading her Bible and going through her study notes.

The five-year-old popped in and saw her too, but tip-toed out when she saw Granny so immersed. When the child's Mum asked what Granny was doing, 'Oh!' came the reply, 'she's swotting for her finals'!

★   ★   ★

'Of course, on the other hand, . . .'

★   ★   ★

Whilst the vicar was showing a group of children around his old parish church, they came to a big plaque on the wall containing the names of men and women who had died during two world wars. 'What are those names?' asked a child. 'They are the names of those who have died in the services,' said the vicar. 'Was it in

9

the morning services or the evening services?' asked the child.

A minister was not having a very good time in his own church, and was not very popular. It was decided that perhaps he needed a short break. He was given the opportunity to see what his denomination's missionaries were doing in an African country, and whilst there he was invited to give a talk to the N'Toto people. The chief of the N'Toto could speak English, so interpreted for him. His talk seemed to go really well. People got very excited as he shared his own brand of theological thought with them. They were far more animated than his congregation at home. Indeed, by the end of his talk they were standing up and shouting excitedly, 'Kabola, Kabola', waving their arms in the air. The preacher understood them to be shouting something like 'Hallelujah' and was uplifted by this experience, and so pleased with the reception he got. After the service his interpreter led him to his hut across a muddy field, where cows had obviously been grazing, and left their characteristic mark. Kindly he said to the preacher, 'Be careful, and don't step in the Kabola'!!

'Quick, call the doctor, Johnny's swallowed a coin.' 'No I'll call the Rector, he can get money out of anybody.'

Fast food is what Christians eat in Lent.

What do they call pastors in Germany? German Shepherds.

A group of boys at school were arguing about whose dad got paid the most. One boy's dad was a lorry driver, one boy's dad was a computer salesman, and one boy's dad was a vicar. The argument was ended when the vicar's son said, 'Well, it takes four men carrying four large plates full of money to carry my dad's wages each week.' No one could better that!

There was a competition between the clergy of a certain town. When the Bishop drove up to a petrol station in his Jag, an Elder from the charismatic church also drew up in his mini-van. They knew each other vaguely because they had been in meetings together.

Elder to Bishop: Have you got stereo sound in there?
Bishop: No, I've got quadraphonic sound.
Elder: So have I.
Elder: Have you got a TV in there?
Bishop: I have.
Elder: So have I.
Elder: Have you got a double bed in there?
Bishop: No.
Elder: I have.

The Bishop was mad that the Elder had got a double bed and he hadn't, so he got one fixed, at great cost to the diocese.

Soon afterwards he saw the Elder's mini-van parked by the side of the road, the windows all steamed up.

The Bishop decided to show off his new double bed, so he knocked at the window of the mini-van. No answer. He knocked again. Eventually the window slowly opened and the Elder's head appeared. The Bishop proudly explained that he now had a double bed in the back of his Jag.

The Elder was astounded. 'Do you mean that you've dragged me out of the bath just to tell me that!'

★   ★   ★

★   ★   ★

The Pope arrives in the UK and is being driven to the Houses of Parliament. The car is a limousine with dark glass windows. When they are about a mile from Parliament, the Pope asks the chauffeur to let him drive the last mile because he has never driven a right-hand-drive car and would like to see what it is like. After some persuading, the driver lets him drive. They arrive at the gates of Parliament, and the Pope rolls down his window as the policeman comes over to the car. The policeman stops short, gestures to the Pope to wait a minute, and rushes back to his phone. His sergeant answers and the conversation goes like this:

Policeman: Could you send someone important down to the front gates?

Sergeant: Do you want me to come down?

Policeman: No, is there anyone more important around?

Sergeant: I could get a minister out of the House, I suppose.

Policeman: Is there nobody even more important available?

Sergeant: I could get the Prime Minister at a push, I suppose.

Policeman: I need someone more important than that!

Sergeant: Only the Queen is more important. For goodness sake, who on earth have you got down there?

Policeman: I don't know who I've got, but the Pope's driving him!

★　　　★　　　★

Four ministers went on a retreat, sat in a room and decided to confess their weaknesses.

1st Minister: My problem is, there are too many beautiful women in the world.

2nd Minister: My problem is drinking too much.

3rd Minister: My problem is I tell lies. Last week I

was about to be caught for speeding, so I just put on my collar and said I was taking a funeral. Works every time.
4th Minister: I am very sorry to have to tell you my problem – I gossip and I am not able to stop it.

★   ★   ★

A couple had two little boys, aged 8 and 10, who were excessively mischievous. They were always getting into trouble and their parents knew that, if any mischief occurred in the town, their sons were probably involved.

The boy's mother heard that a clergyman in town had been successful in disciplining children, so she asked if he would speak with her boys. The clergyman agreed, but asked to see them individually. So the mother sent her 8-year-old first, in the morning, with the elder boy to see the clergyman in the afternoon.

The clergyman, a huge man with a booming voice, sat the younger boy down and asked him sternly, 'Where is God?'

The boy's mouth dropped open, but he made no response, sitting there with his mouth hanging open, wide-eyed. So the clergyman repeated the question in an even sterner tone, 'Where is God!!?' Again the boy made no attempt to answer. So the clergyman raised his voice even more and shook his finger in the boy's face and bellowed, 'WHERE IS GOD?'

The boy screamed and bolted from the room, ran directly home and dived into his closet, slamming the door behind him. When his elder brother found him in the closet, he asked, 'What happened?'

The younger brother, gasping for breath, replied, 'We are in BIG trouble this time. God is missing – and they think we did it!'

A rabbi, a priest and a pastor were all in a boat together fishing. The pastor said to the others, 'I think I am going to go over to that shore and sit down.'

So, he got out of the boat, walked across the water and sat down on the shore.

Then the priest said to the rabbi, 'I think I am going to go over there to join him.'

So, he did the same as the pastor and sat next to him on the shore.

The rabbi thought to himself, 'Well, if they can do it, so can I!'

So, he climbed out of the boat, but immediately fell in the water. The pastor turned and said to the priest, 'Do you think we should have told him where the rocks were?'

A provincial vicar went to London to order a banner for the Sunday School, and realised he had left the details behind. He sent home asking for the instructions about the words and size to be cabled to him. The messenger boy grinned as he brought the telegram reading, 'UNTO US A SON IS BORN TWELVE FOOT LONG BY NINE FOOT WIDE.'

'What's in this bottle?' the Customs official asked the priest.

'Holy Water,' he replied.

'It smells like whisky to me.'

'Praise the Lord, another miracle!'

The great comedian Sir Harry Secombe was known for cracking gags in every situation. Even at his funeral the mourners couldn't help wondering if he would suddenly sit up in his coffin and blow one of his famous raspberries.

Once, when Harry was filming one of his *Highway* programmes for the long-running television series, he was waiting for his guest to arrive. As he stood at the front of the church, the doors at the back opened, and fellow comedian Billy Dainty appeared. Noticing Harry had seen him arrive, Billy made his way down the aisle with one of his infamously funny walks.

As he approached the front of the church, Harry immediately remarked, 'He moves in mysterious ways, you know!'

A preacher went to his church office on Monday morning and discovered a dead mule in the churchyard. He called the police. Since there did not appear to be any foul play, the police referred the preacher to the health department. They said since there was no health threat that he should call the sanitation department. The sanitation manager said he could not pick up the mule without authorization from the mayor.

Now the preacher knew the mayor and was not too eager to call him. The mayor had a bad temper and was generally hard to deal with, but the preacher called him anyway. The mayor did not disappoint. He immediately began to rant and rave at the pastor and finally said, 'Why did you call me anyway? Isn't it your job to bury the dead?' The preacher paused for a brief prayer and asked the Lord to direct his response. He was led to say, 'Yes, Mayor, it is my job to bury the dead, but I always like to notify the next of kin first!'

★ ★ ★

Hilary found that Jean was wearing the same outfit.

A drunk stumbles along to a baptismal service on a Sunday afternoon down by the river. He proceeds to tumble down into the water and stands next to the minister. The minister turns, notices the old drunk and says, 'Mister, are you ready to find Jesus?'

The drunk looks back and says, 'Yes sir, I am.'

The minister then dunks the fellow under the water and pulls him right back up.

'Have you found Jesus?' the minister asks.

'No, I didn't!' says the drunk.

The minister then dunks him under for quite a bit longer, brings him up and says, 'Now brother, have you found Jesus?'

'No, I did not!' says the drunk again.

Disgusted, the minister holds the man under for at least 30 seconds this time, brings him up and demands, 'For the grace of God, have you found Jesus yet?'

The old drunk wipes his eyes and pleads, 'Are you sure this is where he fell in?'

Holy Help

Heaven touches earth with a smile

God has brought me joy and laughter
Genesis 21 v 5

God speaks to his creation in a myriad of ways, and sometimes one can almost imagine a grin on his face.

A man was taking it easy, lying on the grass and looking up at the clouds. He was identifying shapes when he decided to talk to God.

'God,' he said, 'how long is a million years?'

God answered, 'In my frame of reference, it's about a minute.'

The man asked, 'God, how much is a million pounds?'

God answered, 'To me, it's a penny.'

The man then asked, 'God, can I have a penny?'

God answered, 'In a minute.'

Top Ten Reasons Why Eve Was Created

10. God was worried that Adam would frequently become lost in the garden because he would not ask for directions.

9. God knew that one day Adam would require some-one to locate and hand him the remote.

8. God knew Adam would never go out and buy him-self a new fig leaf when his wore out and would therefore need Eve to buy one for him.

7. God knew Adam would never be able to make a doctor's, dentist's or haircut appointment for him-self.

6. God knew Adam would never remember which night to put the rubbish out on the pavement.

5. God knew that if the world were to be populated, men would never be able to handle the pain and discomfort of childbearing.

4. As the Keeper of the Garden, Adam would never remember where he left his tools.

3. Apparently, Adam needed someone to blame his troubles on when God caught him hiding in the garden.

2. As the Bible says, it is not good for man to be alone!

And the one big reason why God created Eve . . .

1. When God finished the creation of Adam, he stepped back, scratched his head, and said, 'I can do better than that!'

There once was a flood and everyone had reached safety except for one man. He climbed to the top of his house, with the water lapping at his feet. A helicopter flew over his head and hung down a rope for him to climb, but the man was deeply religious and said, 'It's all right! The Lord will save me!'

So the helicopter flew away. The water continued to rise and a boat came to him but, once again, the man shouted, 'No! Go AWAY! The Lord will come and save me!'

And, once again, the boat sped off.

The water was getting dangerously deep by now so the helicopter came back and, on cue, the man repeated, 'I don't need saving! My Lord will come.'

Reluctantly, the helicopter left.

The rain continued to pour down, the water continued to rise, the flood overwhelmed everything, and the man drowned.

At the gates of Heaven, the man met St Peter. Confused, he asked, 'Peter, I have lived the life of a faithful man – why did my Lord not rescue me?'

St Peter replied, 'For pity's sake! He sent you two helicopters and a boat! What more did you want?'

★   ★   ★

Kevin took himself off to his study to pray for peace.

Mr Thompson hit seventy and decided he wanted to live a long time. He started to diet and exercise, and even gave up smoking. He lost his paunch, his body firmed up, and to make the picture complete, he bought a toupee to cover his bald scalp. Then he walked out into the street and was hit by the first car that came along. As he lay dying, he looked heavenward and called up, 'God, how could you do this to me?' God answered, 'To tell you the truth, I didn't recognize you!'

God was very pleased with the way that Noah had obeyed him in building the ark. Noah's silly daughter noticed this and asked him if he could do it again.

'Again?' enquired Noah.

'Yes, and this time it would be really good to build it eight storeys high,' replied the daughter, 'full of water and filled with fish.'

'Whatever for?' asked the confused Noah.

'Well, I've always wanted a multi-storey carp-park,' came the reply.

One day three men were walking along and came upon a raging, violent river. They needed to get to the other side, but had no way of crossing the river. The first man prayed to God saying, 'Please God, give me the strength, courage, and ability to cross this river.'

Flash! God gave him big arms and strong legs, and he was able to swim across the river in about two hours.

Seeing this, the second man prayed to God saying, 'Please God, give me the strength, courage, and ability to cross this river.' Flash! God gave him a boat and he was able to row across the river in about three hours.

The third man had seen how this worked out for the other two, so he also prayed to God saying, 'Please God, give me the strength, courage, and ability to cross this river.' And flash! God turned him into a woman and he walked across the bridge.

★ ★ ★

Oh, good . . . you're not busy

★ ★ ★

Two travelling angels stopped to spend the night in the home of a wealthy family. The family was rude and refused to let the angels stay in the mansion's guest room. Instead the angels were given a small space in the cold basement. As they made their bed on the hard floor, the elder angel saw a hole in the wall and repaired it. When the younger angel asked why, the elder angel replied, 'Things aren't always what they seem.'

The next night the pair came to rest at the house of a very poor, but very hospitable farmer and his wife. After sharing what little food they had the couple let the angels sleep in their bed, where they could have a good night's rest. When the sun came up the next morning the angels found the farmer and his wife in tears. Their only cow, whose milk had been their sole income, lay dead in the field. The younger angel was infuriated and turned on the elder angel.

'How could you have let this happen? The first man had everything, yet you helped him,' she accused. 'The second family had little but was willing to share everything, and you let the cow die.'

'Things aren't always what they seem,' the elder angel replied. 'When we stayed in the basement of the mansion, I noticed there was gold stored in that hole in the wall. Since the owner was so obsessed with greed and unwilling to share his good fortune, I sealed the wall so that he wouldn't find it. Then last night as we slept in the farmer's bed, the angel of death came for his wife. I gave him the cow instead. Things aren't always what they seem.'

Teenagers!! Whenever your kids are out of control, you can take comfort from the thought that even God's omnipotence did not extend to God's kids. After creating Heaven and earth, God created Adam and Eve.

And the first thing he said to them was: 'Don't!'

'Don't what?' Adam replied.

'Don't eat the forbidden fruit,' God said.

'Forbidden fruit? We got forbidden fruit? Hey, Eve . . . We got forbidden fruit!'

'No way!'

'Yes WAY!'

'Don't eat that fruit!' said God.

'Why?'

'Because I'm your Creator and I said so!' said God, wondering why he hadn't stopped after making the elephants.

A few minutes later God saw the kids having an apple break and was angry. 'Didn't I tell you not to eat that fruit?' God asked.

'Uh huh,' Adam replied.

'Then why did you?'

'I dunno,' Eve answered.

'She started it!' Adam said.

'Did not!'

'DID so!'

'DID NOT!!'

Having had it with the two of them, God's punishment was that Adam and Eve should have children of their own.

★　　　★　　　★

Sometimes it's good to bear in mind that we were all young once . . .

Remember, old folk are worth a fortune. With silver in their hair, gold in their teeth, stones in their kidneys, and gas in their stomachs.

25

I have become a little older since I spoke to you last, and changes have come into my life. I am quite a frivolous old girl; I am seeing five gentlemen each day. As soon as I wake up Will Power helps me get out of bed, then I visit Lou, next it's time for Mr Quaker to give me my porridge.

They leave and Arthur Ritis shows up and stays for the rest of the day, though he doesn't stay long in one place, he takes me from joint to joint.

After such a busy day I'm ready for bed with Johnny Walker.

What a life, and oh yes, I'm flirting with Al Zymer.

The vicar came the other day and said, 'At your age you should be thinking of the here-after'. 'Oh, I do. No matter where I am, in the lounge or upstairs or in the kitchen, I ask myself – now what am I here after?'

★　　★　　★

Bats were not a problem.

Holy Help

There are four people named Everybody, Somebody, Anybody and Nobody. There was an important job to be done and Everybody was asked to do it. Anybody could have done it, but Nobody did. Somebody got angry about that, because it was Everybody's job. Everybody thought that Anybody could do it, but Nobody realised that Everybody wouldn't do it. It ended up that Everybody blamed Somebody when Nobody did what Anybody could have done.

Holy Hiccups

A spiritual slip on a banana skin

Laughter is a tranquilliser with no side effects.
Mercelene Cox

Misunderstandings are a source of great amusement, especially when we put ourselves in the victim's shoes.

A man was preaching in an evangelistic service and made this unfortunate mistake: 'If you are without God tonight you are like a ship with a hole in its bottom. I want you to know that I haven't got a hole in my bottom.'

The vicar reassured the nervous bridegroom that he had no need to memorize anything: 'You repeat all the responses after me.' So when the vicar asked him, 'Do you take this woman to be your wife?' the bridegroom answered, 'After you!'

A bridegroom with a stammer said, 'I'm s-sure my w-wife will be a great ba-boon to me.'

Muslims are allowed four wives, but in the Church of England you are allowed sixteen: four better, four worse, four richer, four poorer.

I married an angel: she flies up in the air at the slightest excuse and is always harping on about something.

Walking into a department store, a man cautiously approached the lingerie counter and spoke shyly to the woman behind it. 'I'd like to buy a bra for my wife.'

'What type of bra?' asked the clerk.

'Type?' enquired the man. 'There is more than one type?'

'Look around,' said the saleslady, as she showed a sea of bras in every shape, size, colour and material. 'Actually, even with all of this variety, there are really only four types of bras.'

Confused, the man asked what the types were.

The saleslady replied, 'The Catholic type, the Salvation Army type, the Presbyterian type, and the Baptist type. Which one do you need?'

Still confused the man asked, 'What is the difference between them?'

The lady responded, 'It is all really quite simple. The Catholic type supports the masses, the Salvation Army type lifts up the fallen, the Presbyterian type keeps them staunch and upright, and the Baptist type makes mountains out of mole hills.'

'After studying our financial records for the past year, we suspect one of you ushers is skimming some of the offerings.'

A nun received a gift of ten pounds, and thinking it conflicted with her vow of poverty, she put it in an envelope with a note reading, 'Don't despair – Sister Angelina', and gave it to a man in shabby clothing whom she had seen standing in the street outside. She was surprised that he took it and walked off without saying anything, but even more surprised when he returned later, and handed her sixty pounds, saying, 'Here's your winnings, Sister. "Don't Despair" came in at five to one.'

Dear Inspector of Taxes, I have recently become a Christian, and now I cannot sleep at night for feeling guilty about the income I failed to declare on my last tax return. I enclose £100, and if I still can't sleep I will send the rest.

A burglar breaks into a house in the middle of the night and sets to work filling his bag with goodies. Suddenly, he hears a voice say, 'Jesus is watching you', and he quickly looks around, scanning the room with his flashlight. Seeing no one there he thinks he simply imagined it, and continues to stuff his bag with loot.

Suddenly he hears the voice again – 'Jesus is watching you'. This time he's sure it comes from within the room, so he slowly shines his flashlight around until he notices a birdcage in the far corner. Moving towards it he sees that there's a parrot in the cage.

'Did you say something?' the burglar asks. 'Yes, I said "Jesus is watching you" because I thought you should be warned,' replies the parrot. 'Well, who are you to warn me?' asks the burglar. 'My name is Moses,' says the parrot. The burglar laughs and says, 'What kind of people would name their parrot Moses?'

'The same kind of people who would name their Rottweiler Jesus!' the parrot replies.

Advice to those looking for a perfect church to join: if you find one, don't join it, because then it won't be perfect any longer.

Some church people are like blisters: they arrive after all the hard work has been done.

* * *

At an evangelists' conference in the USA several ministers were attending their first class on emotional extremes.

'Just to establish some parameters,' said the professor, to the student from Arkansas, 'what is the opposite of joy?' 'Sadness,' said the student.

'And the opposite of depression?' he asked of the young lady from Oklahoma. 'Elation,' said she.

'And you sir,' he said to the young man from Texas, 'how about the opposite of woe?' The Texan replied, 'Sir, I believe that would be giddy-up.'

* * *

A woman went to the Post Office to buy stamps for her Christmas cards. 'What denomination?' asked the clerk.

Holy Hiccups

'Oh, good heavens! Have we come to this?' said the woman. 'Well, give me 50 Catholic and 50 Baptist ones.'

★ ★ ★

'Our speaker tonight is Bob Wilson, a missionary to the city of Memphis.'

★ ★ ★

There was an old Fellow of Trinity,
a Doctor well versed in Divinity,
    but he took to free-thinking,
    and then to deep drinking,
and so had to leave the vicinity. Boom! Boom!

★ ★ ★

There was an Archdeacon who said,
'May I take off my gaiters in bed?'

33

The Bishop said, 'No,
  you must wear them, you know,
right up till the day you are dead.'

To his spouse said a vicar in Sydenham,
'My trousers, now where have you hydenham?
  I admit it is true
  they were not very new,
but I foolishly left twenty quidenham.'

There once was a proud young priest
who lived almost wholly on yeast
  'For,' he said, 'it is plain
  we must all rise again,
and I want to get started, at least.'

A lady was out on her bike running errands for the vicar, when her chain broke. She started to wheel the bike home when a car drew up and offered her a lift back. Unfortunately the car was a Porsche and they were unable to get the bike inside.

'Don't worry,' said the kind driver. 'I've got a rope here and if we tie it on to your bike I can tow you gently home. If you've got a problem just ring your bell and wave your arm and I'll see you in my mirror.'

The old lady warily agreed and the car began slowly

to pull her along the road. Suddenly another car shot past them. It was a BMW.

'I'm not having that!' thought the driver of the Porsche and hitting down into gear shot off at break-neck speed to catch up, with the old lady in tow.

After some while they passed a patrol car in which sat an amazed policeman. 'You'll never guess,' he reported on his radio. 'I've just seen a BMW and a Porsche doing at least 70 followed by an old lady on a bike waving her hands, ringing her bell, trying to get past them both!'

★　　★　　★

★　　★　　★

We out of Static-Guard again, Roy?

★ ★ ★

DON'T QUIT

When things go wrong, as they sometimes will,
When the road you're treading seems all uphill,
When the funds are low and the debts are high
And you want to smile but you have to sigh,
When care is pressing you down a bit,
Rest, if you must, but don't you quit!

Life is queer with its twists and turns,
As every one of us sometimes learns,
And many a failure turns about
When he might have won had he stuck it out;
Don't give up, though the pace seems slow,
You might succeed with another blow.

Holy Hiccups

Often the goal is nearer than it seems,
To a faint and faltering man,
Often the struggler has given up,
When he might have captured the victor's cup,
And he learned too late, when the night slipped
    down,
How close he was to the golden crown.

Success is failure turned inside out,
The silver tint of the clouds of doubt,
And you never can tell how close you are,
It may be near when it seems afar;
So stick to the fight when you're hardest hit,
It's when things seem worse that you mustn't quit!

Holy Hopes

An amusing look at our destiny

**Being cheerful keeps you healthy.
It is slow death to be gloomy all the time.**
Proverbs 17 v 22

*We all have our own idea of what Heaven will be like,
but some suggestions are more peculiar than others!*

———————

A Welsh rugby player turned up at Heaven's gate and was asked by the guardian if there was anything he wanted to confess.

'Well yes,' he replied, 'I have always been in grave doubt about a certain try that I was given credit for in an international match against England. I was given credit for it, but I don't think I really deserved it.'

'Oh, I shouldn't worry about that, I think that can be easily forgotten,' smiled the angel.

'Well that's really, really kind of you, St Peter,' replied the player, firmly shaking his hand.

'No, St Peter's off today,' came the reply. 'I'm St David!'

★   ★   ★

St Peter was patrolling the wall that separated Heaven from Hell, checking for holes, which the people in Hell kept making so that they could try and escape into Heaven. On average he repaired at least twenty a day, and was getting fed up with it all. Spotting a movement a few metres ahead of him he broke into a run and arrived at a hole, which the devil himself was trying to get through yet again.

'I'm fed up with you,' said St Peter. 'Do you realise the trouble you cause me? I have to mend so many holes every day to stop you lot trying to get in here and I've just about had enough.'

The devil's head was poking through the hole and he looked at St Peter and said, 'What do you mean? It's not us lot trying to get in there, but your lot trying to get in with us.'

'Don't be stupid,' said St Peter. 'Why on earth would anybody here in the Utopia of Heaven want to go in with you lot to the fire and brimstone and live in the living hell you have in there? I've had enough of all this anyway, now you mend the hole you've made and get back into your own side and we'll forget all about it this time.'

'The hole was made by your people trying to get in here,' replied the devil, 'so you mend it.'

'Don't talk rubbish,' said St Peter. 'Your people did it, so you mend it.'

This argument went on for ten minutes before the devil finally said, 'Look here. We're obviously not going to agree on this one so I suggest we each get our lawyers to represent us and sort it out for us.'

'OK,' said St Peter, 'I'll mend the hole.'

'You admit your guys made the hole then,' said the devil.

'No, not at all,' said St Peter, 'but you know as well as I do that I'm never going to find a lawyer in here.'

A woman found herself standing at the Pearly Gates. St Peter greeted her and said, 'These are the gates to Heaven, my dear. But you must do one more thing before you can enter.' The woman was very excited, and asked of St Peter what she must do. 'Spell a word,' St Peter replied. 'What word?' she asked. 'Any word,' answered St Peter. 'It's your choice.' The woman promptly replied, 'Then the word I will spell is love. L-O-V-E.' St Peter welcomed her in, and asked her if she would mind taking his place at the gates for a few minutes while he took a break.

Whilst the woman sat in St Peter's chair a man approached the gates, and she realized it was her husband. 'What happened?' she cried. 'Why are you here?' Her husband stared at her for a moment, then said, 'I was so upset when I left your funeral, I got in an accident. Did I really make it to Heaven?' 'Not yet,' she replied, 'you must spell a word first.' 'What word?' he asked. The woman responded, 'Czechoslovakia.'

St Peter asked a new arrival in Heaven how he had got there.

'Flu!' came the reply.

A man dreamt that he had died and gone to Heaven. Arriving at the gates, Peter said that what he should do was to take a six-foot piece of chalk, carry it over his shoulder and go down the marble staircase to the bottom. When he got there he would find a row of chalkboards as far as the eye could see. He was told to find the one with his name on, and then write down everything he had ever done wrong.

He said, 'Thank you', and started off down the staircase. Half way down he met his good friend the vicar coming towards him. 'Hi Vic,' he said, 'where are you going?'

'Back for another piece of chalk!' came the reply.

* * *

He's not counting Wednesday nights!

* * *

In Heaven there were two queues for married men to join. One was for 'henpecked' husbands, and the other was for those who were not henpecked. Underneath the henpecked sign was a very long queue stretching for eternity. Under the other was one man standing totally alone. An angel noticed this and went to speak to the man to ask why he was in that queue.

'My wife told me to stand here,' the man replied.

An 85-year-old couple, having been married almost sixty years, had died in a car crash. They had been in good health the last ten years, mainly due to her interest in health food and exercise. When they reached the Pearly Gates, St Peter took them to their mansion, which was decked out with a beautiful kitchen and master bath suite and jacuzzi. As they 'oohed and aahed' the old man asked Peter how much all this was going to cost. 'It's free,' Peter replied, 'this is Heaven.'

Next they went out to survey the championship golf course that the home backed up to. They would have golfing privileges everyday, and each week the course changed to a new one, representing the great golf courses on earth. The old man asked, 'What are the green fees?' Peter's reply. 'This is Heaven, you play for free.'

Next they went to the clubhouse and saw the lavish buffet lunch, with all the cuisines of the world laid out. 'How much to eat?' asked the old man. 'Don't you understand yet? This is Heaven, it is free!' Peter replied with some exasperation.

'Well, where are the low fat and low cholesterol tables?' the old man asked timidly. Peter lectured, 'That's the best part . . . you can eat as much as you like of whatever you like and you never get fat and you never get sick. This is Heaven.'

With that the old man went into a fit of anger, throwing down his hat and stomping on it and shrieking wildly. Peter and his wife both tried to calm him down, asking what was wrong. The old man looked at his wife and said, 'This is all your fault. If it weren't for your stupid fat-free diet, I could have been here ten years ago!'

A minister arriving at a conference sent his wife an e-mail, but it was accidentally sent to a woman who had just lost her husband. It said:

'Hi luv, Arrived safely. Good journey. Nice place. Room prepared as promised, but golly it's hot down here! Love, Hubby.'

'Don't you get it, Baxter? You don't have to do that here.'

St Peter was met at the Pearly Gates of Heaven by an odd looking guy.

'Who are you?' enquired St Peter.

'I'm Dave,' he replied.

'What did you do on earth?' asked the guardian.

'I was a scrap metal merchant in Bradford,' Dave retorted.

'Well you look a bit iffy to me. Wait there while I get you checked out.'

Peter returned five minutes later to find the gates had gone.

A man asked his vicar whether there were any golf courses in Heaven.

'I don't know, but I will ask the Lord in my prayers on Sunday,' suggested the vicar.

A week later, the man saw his vicar and asked if he had a reply to his question.

'Oh yes,' the vicar replied. 'There's good news and bad news. The good news is there are golf clubs in Heaven. The bad news is that you're teeing off in the morning!'

Two Jewish gentlemen were at the Wailing Wall both praying to God. The first one turned to his friend and asked what he was praying for. 'You're not going to believe this,' he replied, 'but my son has just become a Christian.'

'Well you're not going to believe this either,' exclaimed his mate, 'but my son has become a Christian too.'

Just then the heavens opened and God's voice said, 'How can I help you, my sons?'

'Oh dear, oh dear, oh dear. Our two sons have just become Christians!' they both wailed.

God said, 'Well, you're not going to believe this but . . .'

★　　★　　★

I'm getting so old that all my friends in heaven will think I didn't make it.

★　　★　　★

A scruffy looking bloke arrived at Heaven and rang the bell.

'Who are you then?' asked St Peter.

'Wally from Chelmsford,' came the reply.

'And why do you think you deserve to come into Heaven?' asked Peter.

'I've been very brave,' smiled Wally. 'I stood in the middle of Millwall's ground and shouted "Up the Palace!"'

'Goodness,' smirked Peter. 'When was this?'

'Oh, about two minutes ago,' came the reply.

★   ★   ★

Jimmy Cricket sent me a letter from his Mammy, so come closer to this book to read it . . .

'I'm writing with a grieved heart as your Uncle Paddy has just died. You know, son, he was a grand old age altogether. Mind you, the doctor had only given him six months to live. Your father told him to get a second opinion and if the other doctor also gave him six months to live, then he'd have a whole year.

'He's to be buried in the cemetery at the back of the old church. He always said that if God spared him that's where he would want to be buried.'

'Who'd ever have thought you'd need 3-D glasses to see here?'

Holy Hype

The Unauthorized Version

We have a good old laugh at everything and anything, and it always keeps your spirits up.
Harry Secombe

It's amazing what some churches will announce on their advertising boards and in their newsletters in order to lure a bigger congregation.

> The speaker for next Sunday will be found hanging on the notice board in the foyer.

★   ★   ★

Due to the minister's illness, the weekly healing service will be discontinued until further notice.

★   ★   ★

Next week, Deptford Crematorium will be having their annual open day.

★   ★   ★

A notice board read, 'If you're tired of sinning come inside.' Underneath someone had scrawled, 'If you're not, phone 654 3219.'

Driving yourself too hard? Come in for a service! We are even open on Sundays.

As the minister is going on holiday next week, could all Missionary Boxes be handed in to the Manse by Friday evening at the latest.

We regret to announce that the Ladies' Fellowship did not raise any money during their Sponsored Silence this week.

Jumble Sale next Saturday. Ladies, this is a good opportunity to get rid of anything you don't want. Don't forget to bring your husbands.

Persons in this churchyard are forbidden to pick the flowers from any but their own graves.

Trespassers will be forgiven.

A church notice board next to a bus stop read:
Where will you be on Judgement Day?
Under which someone had written:
Still waiting for the number 7 bus, I expect.

The introduction of a computerized spell-checker at this same church meant some words were inadvertently changed in the production of the church newsletter. On the Sunday morning, the congregation solemnly read the words, 'Forgive our trapezes, as we forgive those that trapeze against us.'

A bishop came to preach at a church and found a smaller than usual congregation. 'Did you tell them I was coming?' he asked. 'No,' replied the vicar, 'but the news must have got out somehow.'

'My text for today is the first three words in the Bible . . .
"genuine Moroccan leather."'

Men-tal anxiety . . . Men-opause . . . Men-tal break-
down.
  Ever noticed that all problems start with MEN?

**What do you do with a bachelor who thinks he's God's
gift to women?**
  Exchange him.

Why did God create man before woman?
  Because you're always supposed to have a rough
draft before creating your masterpiece.

'I'd like to thank the board for the lovely plant after our disagreement this week.'

New Christians wanted – no previous experience required.

Why pray when you can worry?

When you get to eternity, will you be in smoking or non-smoking?

AN ALPHABET OF EXCUSES

I'd like to go to church every Sunday, but . . .
  A is the Auntie who will come to tea,
  B is the bed that won't release me,
  C is the car . . . 'We do need fresh air',
  D is the dinner only Mum can prepare,
  E for extremes, too 'high' or too 'low',
  F for my feelings, when they're right I go,
  G is the garden, much nearer God's heart,
  H is my husband who won't play his part,
  I for intruders who sit in my pew,
  J is for jokes which the preacher thinks new,
  K all that kneeling which tires me so much,
  L the old language, it's so out of touch,
  M is for money, they always want more,
  N for new hymn tunes I've not heard before,
  O is for overtime, double on Sunday,
  P for preparing I must do for Monday,
  Q the queer noises from some organ keys,
  R for the radio . . . I worship at ease,
  S is for sermons, as dull as ditch water,
  T for temptations; I don't live as I oughter,
  U for unfriendly, no welcome I find,
  V for the voice of that woman behind,
  W is the weather, too wet or too hot,
  X for eXcuses, I've got such a lot,
  Y for the yells from the kids left behind,
  and Z is the zeal, which is what I can't find.

How come when the pastor does it you call it 'motivating' and when I do it you call it 'nagging'?

Of course, the answer to help us through life's ups and downs is often so simple that we miss it altogether. Pray!

To pray to God is easy
Like a telephone call but free,
His line is always open, try it out and see.
A twenty-four hour service,
You know he's always there,
Tell him all your problems,
Let him know you care.
Tell him that you love him,
Thank him for this day,
Tell him he's terrific,

54

Holy Hype

This is how you pray.
Your Bible is your mobile phone
Lift it up and look.
How can you accept his call
If your phone is off the hook?
He is a caring Father
Who hates to see you fall
So! Do not wait till it's too – late
Go now! And make your call.

Holy Hugs

Out of the mouths of babes

He will fill your mouth with laughter.
Job 8 v 21

A child's innocence can bring about lots of laughter. No wonder we are told that we need to be like children before we can enter Heaven. Perhaps some of the things they misinterpret could be better than the originals?

Noah's wife was called Joan of Ark.

The bishop in his robes had just preached on the Good Shepherd, and pointing to his pastoral staff asked the children, 'And do you know who I am?' One child ventured, 'Little Bo Peep?'

A little boy opened the big and old family Bible with fascination; he looked at the old pages as he turned them. Then something fell out of the Bible and he picked it up, looking at it closely. It was an old leaf from a tree that had been pressed in between the pages.

'Mum, look what I found,' the boy called out.

'What have you got there, dear?' his mother asked.

With astonishment in the young boy's voice he answered: 'It's Adam's suit!'

'Lot's wife was a pillar of salt by day, but a ball of fire by night.'

Ronnie refused to be in the play unless he could be Darth Vader.

A mother was baking a lovely chocolate sponge cake. Her two sons, Peter, aged six, and Simon, aged three, were arguing over who should have the first piece when it was baked. The mother, seeing an opportunity to teach a moral lesson said, 'If Jesus were sitting here with us, he would surely say, "Let my brother have the first piece, I can wait".' Peter turned to his younger brother and said, 'Simon, you can be Jesus.'

'Samson slayed the Philistines with the axe of the Apostles.'

'Mom and Dad, they chose me to be the star of the Christmas play!'

A Sunday School teacher was discussing the Ten Commandments with her five- and six-year-old children. After explaining the commandment about honouring your father and mother, she asked, 'Is there a commandment that teaches us how to treat our brothers and sisters?' Without a moment's hesitation, one small boy said, 'Thou shalt not kill!'

'Moses led the Hebrews to the Red Sea, where they made unleavened bread which is bread without any ingredients.'

'Mummy, we don't have to go back to school after Easter.' 'I'm sure that's not so.' 'Yes it is, Mummy, look where it says on this letter from the teacher, "The school will be closed for Good, Friday"!'

'Dad, did you go to Sunday School when you were a boy?' 'Yes, my son, I always went to Sunday School.' 'Well, I think I'm going to give it up, it's not doing me any good either.'

One small child knelt by the side of his bed and prayed, 'Dear God, You know that the Bible says that you come from dust and go to dust? Well, come and have a look under my bed, because someone's either coming or going! Amen.'

'My agent and I have decided that if I don't get my own dressing
room, you'll have to find yourself a new Mary.'

One child's essay at school read: 'Afterwards, Moses
went up on Mount Cyanide to get the ten amendments.
The first commandment was when Eve told Adam to eat
the apple. But it wasn't the apple that was the problem; it
was the pear on the ground. The fifth commandment is to
humour thy father and mother. The seventh commandment is thou shalt not admit adultery.'

A Sunday School was asked, 'Jesus was a carpenter,
what does a carpenter do?' 'Please Miss, he lays carpets,'
came the small reply.

'The epistles were the wives of the apostles.'

A small boy remarked, 'God must have pins and needles all the time!' When asked why he should think that, he replied, 'Because we keep saying in church that Jesus is for ever sitting on God's right hand.'

Six-year-old Angie and her four-year-old brother Joel were sitting together in church. Joel giggled, sang, and talked out loud.

Finally, his big sister had enough. 'You're not supposed to talk out loud in church.'

'Why? Who's going to stop me?' Joel asked. Angie pointed to the back of the church and said, 'See those men there, by the door? They're hushers.'

For little ones who got bored, there were soft toys and crayons.

'David was a Hebrew king skilled at playing the liar.'

A little boy was overheard praying: 'Lord, if you can't make me a better boy, don't worry about it. I'm having a really good time like I am!'

'A Christian should have only one spouse. This is called monotony.'

The minister took a little girl visiting with him one day. Upon entering a very old lady's home, the child had the audacity to ask the lady how old she was.

'Oooo, I don't know, sweetheart. I'm so old I can't remember.'

'Well, you should look in your knickers then,' came the chirpy reply. 'Cos in mine it says age 3–4!'

'Solomon, one of David's sons, had 300 wives and 700 porcupines.'

'Our Sunday School lesson was about Jordan baptising Jesus in the John.'

Someone had spread it around that Midnight Mass was a horror movie.

'Now Johnny, what word do Christians shout when they are very, very happy?'
    'Bingo!'

A mother was teaching her 3-year-old the Lord's Prayer. For several evenings at bedtime she repeated it after her mother. One night she said she was ready to go solo. The mother listened with pride as she fully enunciated each word, right up to the end of the prayer. 'Lead us not into temptation,' she prayed, 'but deliver us some e-mail, Amen.'

Another day the same prayer went 'Dear God. Harold be thy name. Lead us not to Penge station. Amen.'

'When Mary heard that she was the mother of Jesus, she sang the Magna Carta. Jesus was born because Mary had an immaculate contraption.'

The senior pastor got all the children out to the front to pray for them. Having done that he said, 'Right, what shall we sing?' One little boy put up his hand and said 'Baa Baa Black Sheep.'

'Jesus enunciated the Golden Rule, which says to do one to others before they do one to you. He also explained, "a man doth not live by sweat alone".'

Little girl: 'Mummy, who made Grandma?'
Mummy: 'Why God did, of course.'
Little girl: 'Mummy, who made you?'
Mummy: 'God did.'
Little girl: 'Who made me?'
Mummy: 'God did.'
Little girl: 'He's getting better and better all the time, isn't he?'

'St Paul cavorted to Christianity. He preached holy acrimony, which is another name for marriage.'

A little boy saying his prayers does all the usual thank you's, then says in a very loud voice, 'And don't forget that it's my birthday next week and that I want that new Play Station. Amen.'

His mum looks up in shock and rebukes him. 'You don't have to shout. God is not deaf.'

'No,' came the reply, 'but Granny downstairs is!'

'The people who followed the Lord were called the 12 decibels.'

A teacher asked her pupils what loving-kindness meant. One little boy jumped up and said, 'Please Miss! If I was hungry and someone gave me a piece of bread, that would be kindness. But if they put some jam on it, that would be loving-kindness.'

A friend sent me this poem, to remind us that even as we get older, we must stay 'young at heart':

We met and we married a long time ago.
We worked for long hours when wages were low.
No TV, no wireless, no bath, times were hard,
Just a cold water tap and a walk in the yard.
No holidays abroad, no carpet on the floors,
We had coal on the fire, and we didn't lock doors.
Our children arrived, no Pill in those days,
And we brought them up without any state aid.
They were safe going out, and they played in the park,
And old folks could go for a walk in the dark.
No Valium, no drugs, no LSD,
We cured most of our ills with a good cup of tea.
No vandals, no muggings, there was nothing to rob,
We felt we were rich with a couple of bob.
People were happy in those far off days,
Kinder and caring in so many ways.
Milkman and paperboy would whistle and sing,
A night at the pictures was our own mad fling.
We all get our share of trouble and strife,
We just have to face it, that's the pattern of life.
Now I'm alone I look back through the years,
I don't think of the bad times, the trouble and tears.
I remember the blessings, our home and our love,
And that we shared them together, I thank God above.

Holy Humour

When you've just got to laugh

A joke's not funny till it's been laughed at.
Eric Morecambe

Sometimes you simply don't know why something is funny, it just is.

If the three wise men were women, they would have:

- asked for directions
- arrived on time
- helped deliver the baby
- cleaned the stable
- made a quiche
- and brought more practical gifts

The shepherds by the road are watching the wise men making their way to Bethlehem, and one says, 'Isn't it always the same? You're waiting for a wise man and none come for hours, then all of a sudden three come along at once.'

This isn't so bad . . . last year I was Mary's donkey.

In 1765 *HMS Victory* was built, which fought bravely in the Battle of Trafalgar when Lord Nelson was struck by a cannon ball and died. The sailors were required to scrub the wooden decks using heavy blocks of stone. Being the shape, size and weight of a family Bible, they were nicknamed 'Holystones' and the cleaners called 'Bible-bashers'.

Question: How do you make God laugh?
Answer: Tell him the certainty of your plans for the next six months.

68

The day finally arrives: Forrest Gump dies and goes to Heaven. He is at the Pearly Gates, met by St Peter himself. The gates are closed, however, and Forrest approaches the gatekeeper.

St Peter says, 'Well Forrest, it's certainly good to see you. We have heard a lot about you. I must inform you that the place is filling up fast and we've been administering an entrance examination for everyone. The tests are fairly short, but you need to pass before you can get into Heaven.'

Forrest responds, 'It sure is good to be here, St Peter. I was looking forward to this. Nobody ever told me about any entrance exam. Sure hope the test ain't too hard; life was a big enough test as it was.'

St Peter goes on, 'Yes I know Forrest, but the test I have for you is only three questions. Here is the first: What days of the week begin with the letter T? Second: How many seconds are there in a year? Third: What's God's first name?'

Forrest goes away to think the questions over. He returns the next day and goes up to St Peter to try to answer the exam questions.

St Peter waves him up and says: 'Now that you have had a chance to think the questions over, tell me your answers.'

Forrest says, 'Well, the first one's easy. That'd be Today and Tomorrow.'

The Saint's eyes open wide and he exclaims, 'Forrest! That's not what I was thinking, but . . . you do have a point, and I guess I didn't specify, so I give you credit for the answer. How about the next one?' asks St Peter. 'How many seconds in a year?'

'Now that one's harder,' says Forrest, 'but I thunk and thunk about that and I guess the only answer can be twelve.'

Astounded, St Peter says, 'Twelve! Twelve??! Forrest, how in Heaven's name could you come up with twelve seconds in a year?

Forrest says, 'Shucks, there gotta be twelve: January second, February second, March second . . .'

'Hold it!' interrupts St Peter. 'I see where you're going with this, and I guess I see your point, though that wasn't quite what I had in mind, but I'll give you credit for that one, too. Let's go on with the next and final question: Can you tell me God's first name?'

Forrest replied, 'Andy.'

'OK,' said a frustrated St Peter, 'I can understand how you came up with your answers to my first two questions, but how in the world did you come up with the name of "Andy" as the first name of God?'

'Shucks, that was the easiest one of all,' Forrest replied. 'I learned it from the song . . . "Andy walks with me, Andy talks with me, Andy tells me I am his own . . ."'

Why do only ten per cent of men make it to Heaven? Because if they all went, it would be Hell.

How many counsellors does it take to change a light bulb?

One, but the light bulb must really want to change.

★ ★ ★

A cannibal to another who is cooking a monk in a pot: 'Of course he's not cooked yet, you've been boiling him and he's a friar.'

★ ★ ★

★ ★ ★

An old monk had given the best part of his 89 years to serving God in a monastery. His life-long work had been to translate the original Greek and Latin books for monks into the English language. This had been a painstaking task, making sure that every word and syllable was written with precision and great care.

One day a young novice joined the Order, and after several days watching the older monk, and learning the skills of translating from one language to another, he asked, 'Has anyone ever made a mistake in the transcripts?'

The old monk looked aghast, 'Oh, no!' he replied. 'In fact, I shall go downstairs to the archives and get one of the original books and show you how exact our copy is.'

Several hours had passed by and the younger monk thought, 'I wonder what has become of my elder Brother? Maybe he has tripped over and knocked himself out, or maybe some other malady has come upon him.'

Passing by what seemed to be myriads of dusty old books and papers, he eventually came across the old monk, who was hunched over one of the original scrolls.

'What in Heaven's name is wrong?' asked the young man.

After what seemed an age, the elder monk looked up, and with tears brimming down his cheeks, he uttered the immortal words, 'The original was *celebrate*!'

'God, give me £100,000,' prayed the miser, 'and I'll give ten per cent to the poor. Or if you like you can deduct the £10,000 in advance and just give me £90,000.'

A poor man prayed day after day to win the lottery, and he never won. At last he could stand it no longer and said to God, 'Give me a break, Lord, couldn't you let me win the lottery just once?' The Lord replied, 'Give me a break yourself. Why don't you go out and buy a ticket?'

A Sunday School teacher was versing his tiny flock in the story of the prodigal son. He told the story in very dramatic terms; how the younger son had gone off with all his father's money, how this son had realised what he had done wrong, how he decided to return to his father and beg forgiveness, and how the older son was jealous. At the end of the story, although the children were obviously enthralled, the Sunday School teacher decided to test out their own thoughts on the story.

'So who do you think wanted the son back?' asked the teacher.

'His father,' came the reply.

'Very good,' smiled the teacher. 'So who do you think wasn't pleased to see the son return?' he asked.

'The fatted calf!' came the quick reply.

The bishop saw a vampire and asked his wife what to do. 'Show him your cross,' she answered, so he jumped up and down and said, 'I'm very, very angry with you.'

Two nuns were out shopping in an Austin Mini, and when they could not find a parking place one offered to drive around while the other went into the shops. When she came out she could not see the car, so she asked a passing man, 'Have you seen a nun in a red mini?' The man answered, 'Not since I stopped drinking.'

A true story tells of an old missionary preparing to leave her home in Africa, where she had lived and worked for many years. She asked her 'Diddy', a house servant, if she would like to take something from the house that would remind her about their friendship when she had gone.

'Yes please!' replied the Diddy. 'I'll take your false teeth please!'

'No, you don't understand,' replied the elderly missionary. 'Tell me what you would really like.'

'Your false teeth,' came the reply.

'I'm sure you don't want those. They wouldn't even fit you.'

'Yes I would like them,' insisted the Diddy. 'And yes, they do fit!'

A Scotsman visiting the Sea of Galilee saw a sign for boat trips across the lake for a hundred shekels per person. 'Hoots mon,' he exclaimed, 'if yon's how much it costs, no wonder Jesus walked!'

Holy Humour

A cardinal was asked what he thought about premarital sex. 'I suppose it's OK,' he replied, 'so long as it doesn't make them late for the service.'

I was sent this amazing tongue twister based on the story of the prodigal son:

Feeling foot-loose and frisky, a feather-brained fellow forced his fond father to fork over the farthings. He flew far to foreign fields and frittered his fortune, feasting fabulously with faithless friends.

Finally facing famine and fleeced by his fellows-in-folly, he found himself a feed flinger in a filthy farmyard. Fairly famished, he fain would have filled his frame with foraged food from the fodder fragments.

'Fooey, my father's flunkies fare far fancier,' the frazzled fugitive fumed feverishly, frankly facing facts.

Frustrated by failure and filled with foreboding, he fled forthwith to his family. Falling at his father's feet, he floundered forlornly, 'Father, I have flunked and fruitlessly forfeited family favour.'

But the faithful father, forestalling further flinching, frantically flagged the flunkies to fetch forth the finest fatling and fix a feast.

The fugitive's fraternal fault-finder frowned on the fickle forgiveness of former folderol. His fury flashed, but fussing was futile. The farsighted father figured, 'Such filial fidelity is fine, but what forbids fervent festivity, for the fugitive is found. Unfurl the flags with flaring, let fun and frolic freely flow. Former failure is forgotten, folly forsaken.

'Forgiveness forms the foundation for future fortune.'

The London bus driver's prayer: 'Our Farnham which art in Hendon, Harrow by Rye Lane. Thy Kingston come, Thy Wimbledon, in Erith as it is in Hendon. Give us this day our Leatherhead, and forgive us our bypasses as we forgive those who bypass against us. And lead us not into Thames Ditton, but deliver us from Ewell. For thine is the Kingston, the Purley and the Crawley, for Iver and Iver. Crouch End.'

★　　★　　★

Christmas Cake Recipe
1 cup water
1 cup sugar
4 large eggs
2 cups dried fruit
1 1/2 cups all-purpose flour
1 teaspoon baking soda
1 teaspoon salt
1 cup brown sugar
lemon juice
nuts
1 gallon whisky (Note: Rum may be substituted for whiskey)

Sample the whisky to check for quality. Take a large bowl.

Check the whisky again to be sure it is of the highest quality. Pour one level cup and drink. Repeat.

Turn on the electric mixer; beat 1 cup butter in a large, fluffy bowl.

Add 1 teaspoon sugar and beat again.

Make sure the whisky is still OK. Cry another tup. Turn off mixer.

Break 2 legs and add to the bowl and chuck in the cup of dried fruit.

Mix on the turner. If the fried druit gets stuck in the beaterers, pry it loose with a drewscriver.

Sample the whisky to check for tonsisticity.

Next, sift 2 cups of salt. Or something. Who cares?

Check the whisky.

Now sift the lemon juice and strain your nuts.

Add one tablespoon of sugar or something. Whatever you can find.

Grease the oven. Turn the cake tin to 350 degrees.

Don't forget to beat off the turner. Throw the bowl out of the window. Check the whisky again. Go to bed. Who the heck likes fruitcake anyway?

Little Tim was in the garden filling in a hole when his neighbour peered over the fence.

Interested in what the cheeky-faced youngster was up to, he politely asked, 'What are you up to there, Tim?'

'My goldfish died,' replied Tim tearfully, without looking up, 'and I've just had a funeral service before burying him.'

The neighbour was concerned. 'That's an awfully big hole for a goldfish, isn't it?'

Tim patted down the last heap of earth then replied, 'That's because he's inside your stupid cat.'

★   ★   ★

Noah's family gave him a new nickname after he had finished building his huge boat. They called him an 'Ark-itect'!

★   ★   ★

There was a little old lady who was nearly blind, and she had three sons who wanted to prove which one was the best to her.

The first son bought her a 15-room mansion, thinking this would surely be the best that any of them could offer her.

Her second son bought her a beautiful Mercedes with a chauffeur included, thinking this would surely win her approval.

Her youngest son had to do something even better, so he bought her a parrot that he had been training for 15 years to memorize the entire Bible. You could ask the parrot any verse in the Bible, and he could quote it word for word. What a gift that would be!

The old lady went to the first son and said, 'Son, the house is just gorgeous, but it's really much too big for me. I only live in one room, and it's too large to clean and take care of. I really don't need the house, but thank you anyway.'

Then she confronted her second son with, 'Son, the car is beautiful. It has everything you could ever want on it, but I don't drive and really don't like the chauffeur, so please return the car.'

Next she went to her third boy and said, 'Son, I just want to thank you for your most thoughtful gift. That chicken was delicious.'

A young boy had just received his driving licence. He asked his father, who was a minister, if they could discuss his use of the car.

His father said to him, 'I'll make a deal with you. You bring your grades up, study your Bible a little, and get your hair cut, then we will talk about it.'

A month later the boy came back and again asked his father if they could discuss his use of the car.

His father said, 'Son, I'm really proud of you. You have improved your grades, you've studied your Bible diligently, but you didn't get your hair cut!'

The young man waited a moment and replied, 'You know, Dad, I've been thinking about that. You know Samson had long hair, Moses had long hair, Noah had long hair, and even Jesus had long hair.'

His father replied, 'Yes son, and they walked everywhere they went!'

A friend of mine was coming out of church last Sunday, when the minister stepped forward and, taking him by the hand, took him to one side.

'You need to join the army of the Lord,' the minister said to him.

My friend replied, 'I'm already in the army of the Lord.'

'Then how come I don't see you except at Christmas and Easter,' the minister questioned.

My friend whispered back, 'Because I'm in the Secret Service.'

★　　★　　★

Our congregation is so small that when the minister says 'dearly beloved,' I get embarrassed.

★　　★　　★

A Christian was thrown to the lions in the Colosseum in Rome. He somehow managed to climb out of the arena and ran off down the street. The lion also managed to jump out and gave chase. After about a mile or so, the Christian could run no more so he stopped, got down on his knees and prayed.

'Lord,' said the Christian, 'I can run no more. I ask you, please make this lion become a Christian too.'

Suddenly, before his eyes, a glow comes upon the lion and he too gets down on his knees in front of the Christian, and looking up to Heaven crosses himself and says, 'For what we are about to receive . . .'

A woman who recently became a Christian was burning with her newfound faith. Having attended charismatic churches in the past she found herself in a very traditional little Anglican church for a morning service.

Throughout the service she kept raising her arms in the air calling out 'Alleluia', and 'Praise the Lord' and other such things. When it came to the sermon she became even more animated and noisy. Eventually the vicar looked down at her and asked her if she would please refrain from making so much noise. 'But you don't understand,' she says. 'I have got the Holy Spirit in me!'

'That's as maybe,' says the old priest. 'But you didn't get it here!'

There was an ecumenical service in Ireland – the first that brought Catholics and Protestants together in one community. The Catholic priest came up to the front, followed by three Protestant clergymen. Unfortunately the stage was only set up with one seat, and the protestant clergy stood awkwardly at the back. One of the chief lay people saw what was happening, came up the aisle and whispered in the ear of the rather elderly catholic priest, 'Three chairs for the Protestants.' The priest cleared his throat and announced clearly, 'And now I would like us all to give three cheers for the Protestants ... Hip hip hooray.'

★   ★   ★

'My sermon today is from First Peter, chapter three: "Wives, be subject to your husbands."'

★   ★   ★

A bishop and a headmistress arrived in Heaven at the same time. When the formidable looking teacher was greeted at the gates, she was ushered straight through to one of the best rooms.

The bishop however was sent along a corridor to

much less salubrious surroundings. When the bishop questioned the meaning of this, the heavenly guardian replied, 'My dear Bishop, that woman put the fear of God into more people than you have in a lifetime!'

A pastor, known for his lengthy sermons, noticed a man get up and leave during the middle of his message. The man returned just before the conclusion of the service. Afterwards the pastor asked the man where he had gone.

'I went to get a haircut,' was the reply.

'But,' said the pastor, 'why didn't you do that before the service?'

'Because,' the gentleman said, 'I didn't need one then.'

Jamie and Winnie had just arrived back from holiday, when sadly Jamie suffered a heart attack and died. As the family filed past his open coffin, Granny was heard to say, 'Oh, he looks so peaceful, that holiday must have done him a lot of good!'

There was once a shrimp called Christian whose best friend was a prawn. One day Christian's friend told him how unhappy he was that God had made him a prawn. 'I'd much rather have been a fish,' he declared.

God heard his moan and stretched out his hand across the sea. In an instant the prawn became a tiny little fish and he began to show off his new swimming skills. 'But I liked you the way you were before,' said the shrimp as he watched his friend swim away.

Very soon the prawn got tired of being a fish, and was scared when the bigger fish used to chase him. 'I don't like being a fish,' he moaned. 'Why couldn't God have made me an octopus? I want to be bigger.'

God heard his moans and stretched his hand over the sea. In an instant the fish became an octopus with huge tentacles stretching across the ocean floor.

He was so thrilled with his new body that he swam straight back to his friend to show him. 'What do you think of this then, Christian? Look. I'm an octopus!'

His friend Christian couldn't believe what he saw. 'But I liked you the way you were,' he said as the octopus swam off.

Very soon the octopus got bored once more. 'This is awful,' he complained. 'I keep getting my tentacles caught in the rocks. It might have looked good being an octopus or a fish, but it's not as much fun as being a prawn. I really wish I was back the way I was.'

God heard his moaning, and with a knowing smile stretched out his hand across the sea. In an instant the octopus had become a prawn once more.

He couldn't wait to show his friend that he was back the way he had always been. Swimming as fast as his little arms could take him, he soon arrived at where his friend was sitting on the seabed.

Bursting with excitement he immediately declared that he was back to his old self. Surely his friend would be thrilled. 'Look! Look! I'm back the way I was! I'm a prawn-again-Christian!'

A true story tells of a rather incompetent best man who was on the way to his best friend's wedding by air. Whilst answering a call of nature in the aircraft toilet, he decided to double-check that he still had the ring.

As he held it in his hand and admired its beauty, the plane hit an air pocket and jolted. The ring fell into the toilet pan, and disappeared past the bend. Panicking, the best man stuck his hand into the toilet and round the bend, hoping to locate the lost ring, but without success.

Thinking he could perhaps see the item if he got closer, he stupidly thrust his head into the pan. His head become so securely stuck between the metal ridges of the integrated toilet seat that he was unable to move.

Managing to kick the toilet door with his feet, he attracted the attention of the stewardess. Also unable to release him, she called the pilot, who had to unscrew the top half of the metal toilet system to enable the poor man to stand up, though his head remained trapped within the square metal box.

Having taken so long for the unfortunate man's release, the plane was arriving at its destination and had begun its descent. The embarrassed man was required to take his seat for landing. Gasps and giggles accompanied him as he walked back down the aisle with the metal contraption still on his head.

The airport staff took three hours to cut the man's

head free from its steel entombment. The ring was also recovered, and the best man went happily on his way.

He arrived late for the grand celebratory meal, which had been planned for the night before the wedding, but was relieved that his ordeal was finally over. Now it was important to make a good impression. There would be no more embarrassing moments, he considered.

During the meal, however, a kindly guest quietly pointed out that the best man had forgotten to do up his flies. The grateful man hurriedly rectified the situation, inadvertently catching his zipper in the tablecloth.

At the second course, when the best man got up from the beautifully laid table with as much dignity as he could muster, he walked away carrying the table and its entire contents with him!

It brings a smile to your face when you realise how much things have changed over the years. Some of us were born before television, before penicillin, before polio shots, frozen foods, photocopiers, plastic, contact lenses, videos, computers and the Pill.

We were before credit cards, split atoms, laser beams, foreign holidays and ball-point pens, before dishwashers, washing machines, tumble dryers, electric irons, electric blankets, central heating and drip-dry clothes ... and before Man walked on the moon.

We got married first and then lived together (how quaint can you be?). We thought 'fast food' was what you ate in Lent, a 'Big Mac' was a large raincoat, and a 'bit of skirt' was a cut of beef.

We were before day-care centres, group homes and

disposable nappies. We never heard of FM radio, local radio, tape decks, artificial hearts, yoghurt, and young men wearing earrings. For us 'timesharing' meant togetherness, a 'chip' was a small piece of wood or fried potatoes, 'hardware' meant nuts and bolts, and software wasn't a word.

The term 'making out' used to refer to how you did in your exams, 'stud' was something that fastened a collar to a shirt, and 'going all the way' meant staying on a double-decker bus to the terminus. Pizza, tea bags and instant coffee were unheard of in our day, cigarette smoking was 'fashionable', 'grass' was mown, 'coke' was kept in the coal house, a 'joint' was a piece of meat you had on Sundays, and 'pot' was something you cooked in. Rock music was a grandmother's lullaby, a 'gay' person was the life and soul of the party, and 'Eldorado' was an ice cream.

We who were born so long ago must be a hardy bunch when you think of the ways in which the world has changed and the adjustments we have had to make. No wonder we seem so confused and there appears to be a generation gap today, but by the grace of God and with the ability to laugh, we have survived. Hallelujah!

What does the Bible say about laughter?

There are roughly two types of laughter in the Bible. One is when God scorns humankind and the feeble way in which they attempt to live their lives without him, and the other is a means to bring healing and joy to his creation. Here are some of my favourites. Some passages use laughter to bring confidence and strength, others to illustrate and express stupidity, others as a promise from God that in the midst of difficult times, he is still in charge and that good things are on the way.

However, the first laughter in the Bible came about as a result of one of God's amazing miracles. God had promised the barren Sarah a baby, yet she was 90 at the time! At first, she laughed at the impossibility of the situation, but we know that all things are possible with God, and soon she was literally laughing on the other side of her face.

Sarah said, 'God has brought me joy and laughter. Everyone who hears about it will laugh with me.' Then she added, 'Who would have said to Abraham that Sarah would nurse children? Yet I have borne him a son in his old age.' *Genesis 21 v 6–7*

> The joy that the Lord gives you will make you strong. *Nehemiah 8 v 10*

He will let you laugh and shout again. *Job 8 v 21*

You will laugh at violence and hunger, and not be afraid of the animals. *Job 5 v 22*

. . . They will laugh at you and say, Look, here is the man who did not depend on God for safety. *Psalm 52 v 7*

★   ★   ★

But you laugh at them, Lord; you mock the heathen.
Psalm 58 v 8

How we laughed, how we sang for joy! Then the other
nations said about us, 'The Lord did great things for
them.' Indeed he did great things for us; how happy we
were. *Psalm 126 v 2*

God gives wisdom, knowledge, and happiness to those
who please him. *Proverbs 14 v 13*

Happy are you who weep now; you will laugh! *Luke 6 v 21*

★　　　★　　　★

Four days? Boy! Time sure flies when you're dead!

★　　　★　　　★

When is a brewery mentioned in the Bible?
'Paul stopped at Three Taverns and took Courage.'

When is a press representative mentioned in the Bible?
'Samson took two columns and brought the house down.'

Which is the dentist's verse?
Psalm 81 v 10: 'Open thy mouth wide and I will fill it.'

When is ice-cream mentioned in the Bible?
Walls of Jericho, Lyons of Judah, 'blow up the cornet in the new moon.'

When is tennis mentioned in the Bible?
'Joseph served in the courts of Pharaoh'; 'the Son of Man came not to be served but to serve.'

Who was the greatest financier in the Bible?
Noah. He was floating his stock while everyone else was in liquidation.

Who was the greatest female financier in the Bible?
Pharaoh's daughter. She went down to the bank of the Nile and drew out a little prophet.

Who was the first drug addict in the Bible?
Nebuchadnezzar. He was on grass for seven years.

What kind of motor vehicles are in the Bible?
1. Jehovah drove Adam and Eve out of the Garden in a Fury. 2. David's Triumph was heard throughout the

91

land. 3. The apostles were all in one Accord. 4. A Volkswagen Beetle is mentioned in 2 Corinthians 4 v 8: 'We are pressed on every side, but not crushed.'

What is one of the first things that Adam and Eve did after they were kicked out?
They really raised Cain.

Why was Goliath so surprised when David hit him with a slingshot?
The thought had never entered his head before.

What is the first recorded case of constipation in the Bible?
It's in Kings, where it says that David sat on the throne for forty years.

★   ★   ★

chambers

Index

With special thanks to . . .

All the jokes in this book are new to me, but some I am sure have been around for years and have taken on the cloak of 'Chinese Whispers'. I have credited those who kindly passed on their gags for my collection, but if there are any included here that should be credited to someone unknown to me, please let me know so that I can make the appropriate adjustment in any future edition of this book.

As well as my show business friends, my thanks goes to Steve Cole; Lin Bennett; Steve Fortune; Ruth Mark; Tim Morgan; Mike Elcome; Max Wigley; Mike Spratt; Andrew Taylor; Mike Burn; Charlie Casey; Crawford Telfer; Guy Bennett and Tim Dehn for the loan of their best stories.

I am indebted to IVP for the kind permission to reproduce some of the very funny cartoons from Rob Portlock's *Climbing the Church Walls*, from Mary Chamber's *Church is Stranger than Fiction* and from Rob Sugg's *It Came from beneath the Pew*, and to the Canterbury Press for use of some St Gragoyle's classics from the inimitable 'Ron'.

Special thanks go to Chris Gidney for his inspiration,

encouragement and passion for laughter, and to Michael Counsell for introducing me to so many wonderful stories and for being a priest who can laugh at himself.

I pray that we will not only laugh all the way to Heaven, but carry on laughing with joy when we get there.

All Bible quotations are from the Good News Bible, and are used by permission of the Bible Society.

If you have any funny but true stories of church life you can send them to me at

CIE
PO Box 3019
South Croydon
Surrey CR2 7PJ

I will try to include the best ones in future books.

Christians in Entertainment web site:
www.cieweb.org.uk